Wine

Recipes

Part.1

Mark Mashemanoc

INTRODUCTION

Wine is one of the most treasured and revered of all of the alcoholic beverages. Whether you consider yourself a seasoned wine expert or a novice, wine is truly a luxurious liquid. With the ever-growing popularity of at-home brewing kits for wine lovers, it's no wonder that making your own wine at home has caught on as well.

Making wine is actually pretty easy, with the right stuff, equipment, and sanitizing again and again. You'll need to procure some equipment and some chemicals but don't worry, most of it will last many batches with the proper cleaning and maintaining.

If you can follow a simple recipe, you can make wine. You can make it in the tiniest kitchen apartment. You don't need much specialized equipment. You don't have to be Italian or French or a chemist. You just need a sense of adventure, curiosity, and patience.

Since wine comes in a number of different varieties, you can also try to make different types on your own at home. Each type of wine may take a few different steps or the time it takes to ferment completely may vary.

You can make wine out of anything, even vegetables, so the possibilities are endless. Most people, however, usually use an apple or grape juice base. Fruity wines typically take four to five weeks to make. Another type of wine is called a mulled wine, which is similar to a cider. The difference is that this wine is made with extra additions like cloves and spices and has a heartier taste.

The difference between white wine and red wine comes from whether the skins of the grapes are on or off the wine when it ferments. If you make it at home, you can choose to use red or white grape juice. Chardonnay has more of an apple undertone, and a cabernet sauvignon will usually have elements of blackberry or other rich, dark berries. All in all, most homemade wines take a minimum of three weeks to no more than six weeks to ferment.

Welcome to wine making!

HONEY WINE (MEAD)

1. Bochet

Equipment:
- Very large pot for boil (four- to five-gallon capacity)
- Primary and secondary fermentation vessels
- Plug with hole
- Airlock
- Plug with no hole
- Stirring spoon
- Gloves
- Goggles or other protective eyewear

Ingredients:
- 1.4 gallons water
- 2–3 lbs honey (local, but cheap)
- 1 packet Lalvin EC-1118 or Lalvin D-47 yeast
- 1 tsp yeast nutrient
- $\frac{1}{2}$ tsp yeast energizer

Process:
1. Pour one gallon of your brew water into the pot and mark where the water hits.
2. Pour the water out.
3. Pour the honey into the pot and heat over medium-high heat. Stir as the honey heats. It will bubble and expand considerably. Honey is extremely hot and volatile. Once the boil starts, turn down the heat so that it is boiling, but not splattering out of the pot.
4. When the honey forms bubbles that spit steam when they burst, remove from heat. You can't turn off the heat too early, so err on the side of caution as you start out.
5. Put on gloves and goggles.
6. Add water to the honey carefully—the mixture will splatter.
7. Continue to boil until the must reduces to one gallon, as marked on your pot in Step 1.
8. Pour into carboy, add yeast, and continue as in the base recipe.

2. Morat

Equipment:
- Pot
- Primary and secondary fermentation vessels
- Plug with hole
- Airlock
- Plug with no hole
- Stirring spoon

Ingredients:
- 2 lbs honey (local, but cheap)
- 1 gallon water, divided
- 1/2 tsp yeast nutrient
- 1 packet Lalvin D-47 yeast
- 3 lbs mulberries (cleaned, sorted, frozen; thawed overnight and crushed the night before racking to secondary)

Process:
1. Combine honey, a half gallon of water, and yeast nutrient. Heat to 160°F and maintain for thirty minutes. Skim and remove any foam that collects.
2. Remove from heat and cool to 80°F. Funnel into your one-gallon glass carboy and pitch the yeast according to directions. Pop on your airlock.
3. Fermentation should start within a few days. When it has slowed, siphon into your secondary. Add thawed, crushed mulberries.
4. Put the airlock back in and monitor. When fermentation stops, rack again and store for two to four months.

3. Acerglyn

Equipment:
- Pot
- Primary and secondary fermentation vessels
- Plug with hole
- Airlock
- Plug with no hole
- Stirring spoon

Ingredients:
- 2 to 2½ lbs light honey (I used clover)
- 2 quarts maple syrup
- Acid to taste
- Pasteur champagne yeast

Directions:

1. Bring honey and maple syrup to boil in enough water to liquefy.
2. Add acid.
3. Skim for a minute or two.
4. Cool to at least 70°F.
5. Add water to make you must. Should have a starting gravity of 1.120
6. Pitch with working Pasteur champagne yeast. Should have moderate-vigorous fermentation
7. Rack off after primary fermentation, and once again if it isn't clear in a few more weeks.
8. If the yeast isn't settling after the first fermentation, top off carboy with boiled water.

4. Capsicumel

Equipment:
- Pot
- Primary and secondary fermentation vessels
- Plug with hole
- Airlock
- Plug with no hole
- Stirring spoon
- Rubber gloves
- Straining bags

Ingredients:
- 2½ lbs light honey, divided
- 7½ pts water
- 16 medium-sized jalapeños
- 1 lb golden raisins, chopped or minced

- $1\frac{1}{2}$ tsp acid blend
- $\frac{1}{4}$ tsp grape tannin
- $\frac{3}{4}$ tsp yeast nutrient
- $\frac{1}{2}$ tsp pectic enzyme
- 1 packet Pasteur champagne yeast
- $\frac{1}{2}$ tsp potassium sorbate
- Campden tablet, crushed

Directions:

1. Mix 2 lbs honey into water and bring to boil. Boil twenty minutes, skimming off any scum that forms.
2. While boiling, wear rubber gloves to wash jalapeños and cut off stems. Slice lengthwise and remove seeds. Place peppers in blender or food chopper with two cups water and chop coarsely. Set aside.
3. Chop or mince raisins. Put raisins in nylon straining bag and, over primary, pour chopped jalapeños in with raisins. Tie bag and leave in primary.
4. Add acid blend, tannin, and yeast nutrient.
5. Pour honey water over ingredients and stir. Cover primary and set aside until room temperature.
6. When room temperature, add pectic enzyme, cover, and set aside twelve hours.
7. Add yeast and cover.
8. Stir daily until vigorous fermentation subsides (seven to ten days). Wearing rubber gloves, squeeze nylon bag over primary, then discard contents of bag. Transfer liquid to secondary, top up, and fit airlock.

9. Ferment to absolute dryness (sixty to ninety days). Rack into clean secondary, top up, and refit airlock.
10. Rack twice more, forty-five days apart.
11. Stabilize with potassium sorbate and crushed Campden tablet (stirred well), wait fourteen days, then add $\frac{1}{2}$ cup of light, clear honey and stir well to dissolve. Taste. If heat is too strong, add $\frac{1}{4}$ cup of honey and stir well. Taste again. Add additional honey if required.
12. Wait another thirty days and rack into bottles. Age at least six months. Will improve to two years

5. Sima

Equipment:
- Pot
- Primary and secondary fermentation vessels
- Plug with hole
- Airlock
- Plug with no hole
- Stirring spoon

Ingredients:
- 1¼ gallons boiling water
- 2–3 lemons
- ½ cup white sugar
- ½ cup brown sugar
- ½ tsp dry Premier Cuvée yeast
- 3 raisins per bottle (at bottling)

Directions:
1. Bring water to a boil.

2. As water heats, scrub the lemons. Grate the zest from the lemons and set it aside in a small bowl.

3. Peel or cut off the pith (the white part of the peel). Slice or chop the flesh of the lemons, removing the seeds as you go, and add to the bowl of zest.

4. When the water is boiling, reduce the heat and add the sugars and lemon parts. Stir until sugar is fully dissolved.

5. Remove from heat and let sit until room temperature.

6. Transfer everything to your fermenter, including the lemon flesh and zest. Add yeast.

7. Seal with an airlock and leave at room temperature for forty-eight hours.

8. Fill each bottle and add raisins.

9. When the raisins rise to the top of the liquid, the sima is ready to drink.

6. Rhodomel

Equipment:
- Pot
- Primary and secondary fermentation vessels
- Plug with hole
- Airlock
- Plug with no hole
- Stirring spoon

Ingredients:
- 15 lbs alfalfa honey
- 1 gallon water, divided
- 1.5 pint dried rose petals
- $\frac{1}{4}$ tsp citric acid
- $\frac{1}{2}$ tsp tannin

- 1 tsp yeast nutrient
- 1 packet champagne yeast

Directions:
1. Boil honey and one quart of water for ten minutes, skimming off foam.
2. Place petals, citric acid, and tannin in a one-gallon glass carboy. Use the funnel to add the honey water.
3. Add water to make one gallon. When the must is between 75°F and 80°F, add nutrient, sprinkle the yeast on top of the must, and put the airlock on the top of the carboy. Allow to sit for seven to ten days.
4. After seven to ten days, siphon the must into another carboy and ferment until clear.
5. Bottle and age for at least six months.

7. Cyser

Equipment:
- 1 gallon glass carboy
- Airlock
- Stopper with hole

Ingredients:
1½ lbs clover honey
- 1½ lbs wildflower honey
- 1 gallon cider
- 2 Campden tablets
- 1 packet ale yeast

Directions:
1. Mix everything except the yeast.
2. Let sit in fermenter with airlock for twenty-four hours.
3. Add yeast.

4. Rack to secondary when fermentation slows. Allow to age at least three months. Six months of aging is optimal.

CIDER

8. Basic Cider Recipe

Equipment:

- 1-gallon carboy with cap
- Funnel
- Stopper with airlock
- Hydrometer
- Fermometer (stick-on thermometer)
- Bottle filler
- 3 feet plastic tubing
- Auto-siphon racking cane
- Bottle capper
- 10 caps (never reuse)
- 10 bottles (save empties)

Ingredients:
- 1 oz Campden tablets

- 1 gallon apple juice (press local apples fresh yourself for the best results)
- 1 oz pectic enzyme7
- $\frac{1}{2}$ tsp champagne yeast8 (feel free to experiment once you get the process down)
- 1 oz organic corn sugar9
- $\frac{1}{2}$ cup water

1. The night prior to brewing, crush a Campden tablet in about a tablespoon of water and set aside.
2. Prepare a clean working area in the room where you brew.
3. Clean and sanitize your equipment.
4. Use your funnel to pour one gallon of room temperature apple juice into your glass carboy.
5. If your juice is unfiltered, add one ounce of pectic enzyme. You can skip this step if you start with clear apple juice or don't mind a hazy look.
6. Add crushed Campden tablet.
7. Float 1/4 to 1/2 a teaspoon of champagne yeast on top of the juice for a few minutes. This should activate the yeast. After at least three minutes, swirls the bottle to mix. If you wish, place the sanitized cap on the bottle to give it a good shake. Just make sure it's sanitized!
8. Place the sanitized stopper and airlock on the carboy.
9. If you haven't already, place the Fermometer on the outside of the carboy. Place the jug in a warm place where it is shielded from light and able to stay warm, preferably between 55 and 75°F.

10. Allow to sit, mostly undisturbed, for thirty days. During the first week you should see lots of activity: the liquid will churn and foam and your airlock will be bubbling. It's okay if this doesn't last a full week. If you don't see activity, consider activating and pitching a little extra yeast.

11. After thirty days, check the airlock. There should be little to no activity (one bubble or fewer per five-minute span). If you're seeing little to no activity, it's time to bottle.

12. Sanitize your bottles, caps, bottle capper, tubing, auto siphon, and bottle filler.

13. Connect one end of your tubing to the bottle filler and the other to the auto siphon.

14. Fill bottles, being careful to keep the siphon above the sediment at the bottom of the carboy.

15. Store for three to six months before sampling, especially if you carbonate your cider.

9. Cyser (A Cider/Mead Hybrid)

Equipment:
- 1 gallon glass carboy
- Airlock
- Stopper with hole

Ingredients:
- 1½ lbs clover honey
- 1½ lbs wildflower honey
- 1 gallon cider
- 2 Campden tablets
- 1 packet ale yeast

Directions
1. Mix everything except the yeast.
2. Let sit in fermenter with airlock in a warm, dark location for twenty-four hours.
3. Add yeast.
4. Rack to secondary when fermentation slows.

5. Bottle.

6. Allow to bottle age for at least three months. Six months is ideal.

10. Draft Cider

Directions
Follow the basic recipe with the following modifications:
1. Use sweet apples with low acidity. Most grocery store varieties meet this standard.
2. Do not carbonate.
3. Do not add any extra sugars.
4. Keep the ABV below 6%

Directions

Follow the base recipe with the following modifications:

1. Use crab apples or other more tannic varieties.
2. Do not use any yeast.
3. Do not filter, clarify, or carbonate.

This cider relies on natural yeast, so you will not use any yeast other than that found on the apples. You'll need to pick, press, and juice these apples yourself, or ask for a local orchard to press them for you. The apples should be very ripe before pressing.

4. The juice base cannot be pasteurized or have any additives, because they will kill the natural yeast. For this reason, you must use an orchard you trust to avoid using unsafe materials—apples that have been sitting for a long time or have more brown spots than normal. This recipe is best if you can grow and monitor the apples you use yourself.

11.   French-Style or Cidre

Equipment:
- 2 glass carboys
- stopper with hole and airlock
- food storage containers
- funnel
- siphon
- bottler
- bottles made for carbonated beverages
- caps

Ingredients:
- 20 lbs tannic apples (sharps and bitters)
- 1 Campden tablet; crushed
- 1 packet champagne yeast

Directions
1. Sanitize food storage containers (including lids).

2. While food storage containers are soaking, wash and mill apples.

3. Place pulp in food storage containers and allow sitting for at least 24 hours. During this time the apples oxidize.

4. Press the juice out of the apples. Funnel juice and crushed Campden tablet into carboy topped with a stopper and airlock, and allow to settle in a cool, dark place. Check, starting at day 5.

5. You want a brown gel film to form at the top of the liquid. If the film is white you'll need to start over—white means fermentation was too early and quick.

6. On day 7, if you have a brown film, carefully siphon the clear liquid sitting between the brown top and sediment at the bottom into a sanitized carboy.

7. Add $\frac{1}{4}$ teaspoon of yeast and top carboy with a rubber stopper and airlock. Store for at least 30 days before bottling

12.   Ice Cider

Follow the basic recipe with the following modifications:

1. Freeze five gallons of fresh pressed apple juice or cider in a cleaned and sanitized PET carboy.
2. Slowly allow it to melt and separate the juice from the ice. Do this by placing the PET carboy over a sanitized barrel to collect the juice.
3. Ice cider is a difficult fermentation, so make sure to use yeast nutrient even if you usually skip it when making cider.

HERBAL WINE

13.   Cilantro Wine

Equipment:
- 2 pots
- Primary and secondary fermentation vessels
- Drilled bung
- Airlock
- Smooth cutting board
- Knife
- Soup spoon

Ingredients:
- 1 gallon water

- 6–8 cups fresh cilantro
- 1 packet champagne yeast
- 2 lbs sugar
- Yeast energizer (optional)
- Yeast nutrient (optional; you can also use raisins or a squirt of lemon juice)

Process:
1. Pour the gallon of water into a pot, cover it, and turn on the heat.
2. While the water heats, lay the herbs out on a smooth cutting board and bruise them using a soup spoon.
3. Once the water boils, remove from heat and add the bruised herbs. Cover again and allow to steep for at least two days.
4. After two days, remove the yeast from the fridge and set on the counter, allowing it to warm to room temperature.
5. Clean and sanitize a carboy, the carboy cap, bung, airlock, sieve, funnel, ladle, and small drinking glass. If you're using a regular thermometer instead of an adhesive thermometer, make sure to clean and sanitize that, too.

6. When your equipment is ready, strain the tea into the second pot to remove the herbs.
7. Boil the tea and then remove from heat. Stir in the sugar to make your wort. Ladle a small amount into a drinking glass or other small container.

8. Allow the wort to cool to 80°F. Add yeast to the wort in the drinking glass. Wait until it's working (about ten minutes; you'll know when it's foaming or fizzing) and then funnel into the carboy. Funnel the rest of the wort into the carboy over the yeast mixture.

9. Place the sanitized carboy cap on the carboy and give everything a really good shake to oxygenate.

10. Remove the cap and replace with the drilled bung and airlock. Place in a stable environment safe from light for thirty days. Some herbal wines are done fermenting in the primary very quickly, as soon as five days. Feel free to check early, and if fermentation has gotten so slow that you've got fewer than one bubble a minute, go ahead and rack to secondary.

11. Check for fermentation. If bubbles appear in the airlock at a rate of more than one per minute, wait a few more days. Otherwise, clean and sanitize a second carboy, drilled bung and airlock, and the equipment you will use to rack from primary to secondary.

12. Allow your herbal wine to sit for thirty to sixty days in secondary before bottling.

13. Allow the bottled wine to age at least three months before tasting.

14. Don't forget to keep tasting notes so that you can drink future batches at their best.

14.　　Basil Wine

Equipment:
- 2 pots
- Primary and secondary fermentation vessels
- Drilled bung
- Airlock
- Smooth cutting board
- Knife
- Soup spoon

Ingredients:
- 1 gallon water
- 3-4 cups of fresh basil
- 1 packet champagne yeast
- 2 lbs sugar
- Yeast energizer (optional)
- Yeast nutrient (optional; you can also use raisins or a squirt of lemon juice)

Process:

1. Boil the water, covered.

2. While the water heats, bruise the basil leaves and stems. Basil is a soft-stemmed plant and doesn't require destemming. It's also incredibly flavorful, which means you can try skipping the bruising step if you find your basil wines come out too strong. Another option is to bruise some of the basil but not all of it.

3. Remove the boiling water from the heat and add the basil. Allow to steep for two days.

4. After two days, remove the yeast from the fridge and set on the counter, allowing it to warm. Remember, you don't want to shock your yeast, so allow it to warm up for two to three hours.

5. Clean and sanitize a carboy, the carboy cap, bung, airlock, sieve, funnel, ladle, and small drinking glass. If you're using a regular thermometer instead of an adhesive thermometer, make sure to clean and sanitize that, too.

6. Strain the tea and then bring to a boil.

7. Remove the tea from the heat and stir in the sugar. Remove some wort to a small, sanitized drinking glass and add yeast when it's about 80°F.

8. Let the yeast start working. This takes about ten minutes. The yeast is working when you notice bubbles or foam appearing.

9. Funnel the small sample of active yeast and wort into the carboy. Funnel the rest of the wort into the carboy over the yeast mixture.

10. Cover the carboy with its cap and shake it up to oxygenate.

11. Remove the cap and replace with the drilled bung and airlock. Place in a stable, dark environment and monitor. Check your airlock and once primary fermentation slows, rack to secondary. Your wine is ready to be transferred when bubbles appear at a rate of fewer than one per minute.

12. Because basil wine takes a while, consider racking every month for three months before bottling.

13. After bottling the wine, allow it to age at least three months before trying. Keep good notes on tasting. Once you get your basil wine right, you'll want to make more to share and enjoy with friends. Good notes will help you figure out the perfect time to drink it.

15.   Parsley Wine

Equipment:
- 2 pots
- Primary and secondary fermentation vessels
- Drilled bung
- Airlock
- Smooth cutting board
- Knife
- Soup spoon

Ingredients:
- 1 gallon water
- 6-8 cups fresh parsley, bruised
- 1 packet champagne yeast
- 2 lbs sugar
- Yeast energizer (optional)
- Yeast nutrient (optional; you can also use raisins or a squirt of lemon juice)

Process:
1. Boil the water, covered. While it heats, lay out and bruise the parsley using a soup spoon, flat edge of a knife, or kitchen mallet.
2. Once the water is boiling and the parsley is sufficiently bruised, remove the pot of water from the heat and add the parsley. Cover and allow the tea to steep for at least two days.
3. On brewing day, remove the yeast from the fridge and allow it to warm up for two to three hours to avoid shocking it when pitching. Clean and sanitize the equipment while the yeast is warming up to room temperature.
4. Strain the tea into a pot, squeezing to get as much of it as possible.
5. Boil the tea and then remove from heat. Stir in the sugar, making sure it dissolves completely. Ladle some into a small glass or other container.
6. Monitor the temperature of the small glass (it will cool faster than the large pot of tea) and when it reaches 80°F, add the yeast. It will take no more than ten minutes to start working.
7. Funnel the large pot of wort into the carboy and then pitch the active yeast and wort into the carboy.
8. Cap the carboy and give it several vigorous shakes to give the yeast some oxygen.
9. Replace the cap with the drilled bung and airlock. Place in a dark location where it will not experience temperature changes or exposure to light.
10. Check fermentation activity after five days. Once fermentation has slowed to fewer than one bubble

per minute, rack to secondary. Use a drilled bung and airlock. Wait thirty to sixty days before bottling. If there is a lot of sediment after thirty days, re-rack to avoid flaws in the final product.

11. Bottle and allow to age at least three months.

12. Keep tasting notes for future batches.

16.   Beet Wine

Equipment:
- 2 pots
- Primary and secondary fermentation vessels
- Drilled bung
- Airlock
- Smooth cutting board
- Knife
- Soup spoon

Ingredients:
- 1 packet champagne yeast
- 1 lemon, zested and juiced
- 6 whole cloves
- $\frac{1}{2}$ oz shredded ginger

- 1 gallon water, divided
- 3 lbs beets
- 3 lbs sugar
- Yeast energizer (optional)
- Yeast nutrient (optional; you can also use a raisins or a squirt of lemon juice)

Process:

1. Remove the yeast from your fridge and set out to allow it to acclimate to room temperature (about two to three hours).

2. Funnel the lemon juice, cloves, ginger, and half of the water into your carboy.

3. Wash the unpeeled beets very well and dice into $\frac{1}{4}$-inch cubes.

4. Place diced beets and lemon zest in a pot with the rest of the water and bring to a boil, cooking until the beets are tender. Do not overcook—the beets should be tender, not mushy.

5. When the beets are done, add the sugar and stir until completely dissolved. Strain into funnel into the primary fermentation vessel, saving a little in a small glass. Cap and shake the carboy to oxygenate the yeast. (Cooked beets can be eaten or used in soups, etc.)

6. When the reserved wort cools to between 75 to 80°F, add the room temperature yeast. If you're using yeast energizer and nutrient, add it now.

7. Fit the carboy with a drilled bung and airlock. Move carboy to a setting where it will not receive

light and where the temperature will remain stable at the warm end of room temperature. Give it a swirl every day for three days.

8. On the third day, strain into secondary vessel and fit with a drilled bung and airlock.

9.

Monitor regularly. When bubbles reduce to less than one per minute and wort is clear, rack and bottle.

10. Allow to bottle-age for at least one year. According to Jack Keller, this recipe yields a medium-bodied beet wine. If you want a higher-bodied version, increase the beets to four pounds and reduce the sugar used to two.

17.   Blackberry Wine

Equipment:
- Pots
- Primary and secondary fermentation vessels
- Drilled bung
- Airlock
- Bowl
- Fine metal sieve
- Small bottle
- Balloon
- Pin, tack, or straightened paper clip

Ingredients:
- 1 packet champagne yeast
- 1 gallon water
- 4 lbs fresh, ripe blackberries
- 3 lbs sugar

- Yeast nutrient and energizer (optional)

Process:
1. Remove yeast from the fridge so that it can sit out for two to three hours before pitching. Once it has acclimated to room temperature, pitch it in a small amount of water according to the directions on the packet.
2. While the yeast is warming up, start boiling the water.
3. Wash and drain the berries well; shaking them in the colander and washing in batches helps with the removal of excess water. Crush them in a bowl and then transfer to carboy.
4. Funnel the gallon of boiling water into the carboy and mix well.

5. When the mixture is cooled to about 75°F, pitch the active yeast.
6. Fit the carboy with a drilled bung and airlock and set aside for four to five days. Swirl daily. The carboy should be left in a place that is on the warm side of room temperature (70 to 75°F) and away from the light.
7. Add the sugar to the secondary fermentation vessel. Strain the blackberry water through a fine mesh strainer onto the sugar in the secondary. Tap off to the shoulder, the place where the carboy starts to narrow. Reserve the extra. Fit with a drilled bung and airlock.

8. Wrap the carboy with t-shirts or sheets—this wine is very sensitive to light.

9. Take the excess from the primary and place in the small bottle. Pierce the balloon and fit it over the top.

10. Once fermentation has ceased (about a week), add the excess liquor to the larger batch and place in a cool (60 to 65°F), dark place for three months before racking.

11. Allow to sit for another two months, then rack and bottle.

12. Allow to sit for at least six months but up to a year for best flavor.

13. As always, keep notes on your process and the way the wine tastes at different times.

18.　　Ginger Wine

Ingredients:
- 1 gallon water, divided
- 5-6 inches fresh ginger, peeled and grated
- Sliced orange, including the peel and pith
- 4 cups sugar
- 1 packet champagne yeast
- Yeast energizer and nutrient (optional)

Process:
1. Boil one quart of the water.
2. Add the ginger to the water.
3. Add the orange slices, including pith and peel, to the water. Stir, and lower the temperature. Simmer, covered, for at least an hour, adding more water if it loses too much.
4. Strain the tea and return it to the pot.

5. Add the sugar to the hot tea and stir until completely dissolved. Reserve a small amount. Cover the pot and allow wort to cool.

6. When the reserved wort reaches about 80°F add the yeast and allow it to start working. It should take no more than ten minutes.

7. Funnel the large batch of tea into the carboy. If there isn't enough to reach the shoulder of the carboy, top it off with water.

8. When it cools to 80°F, add the activated yeast. Top with a drilled bung and airlock. Store in a stable, warm place where it is out of the light.

9. When fermentation slows to fewer than one bubble per minute, rack to secondary and allow to finish fermentation and clear.

10. Bottle when clear and you have airlock bubbles appearing at a rate of less than 1 per minute. Bottle-age for at least three months.

19.   Rose Petal Wine

Ingredients:
- 6 cups rose petals, pinched at the bottom to avoid vegetal strike
- ¼ cup golden raisins
- 1 gallon water
- 4 cups sugar
- Champagne yeast
- Yeast energizer and nutrient (optional)

Process:
1. Bruise the petals and place in a pot with the raisins.
2. In a second pot, add about two thirds of the water and bring it to a vigorous boil.
3. Remove the water from the heat and stir in the sugar, continuing to stir until completely dissolved.

Then pour into the other pot, over the rose petals. Allow to steep for two hours.

4. Once steeped, remove some of the wort and when it reaches 80°F, add about two thirds of the yeast in the packet. While waiting for the yeast to activate, strain the petal tea into a funnel and the carboy. Top it with the cap or a drilled bung and airlock.

5. When the mixture in the carboy reaches about 80°F, pitch the active yeast. Top with a drilled bung and airlock. Wrap the carboy in tee shirts or a sheet and set in a warm, stable place out of the light.

6. Allow to ferment from five to thirty days, making sure that activity in the airlock has reduced to no more than one bubble per minute. Then rack to secondary and allow to sit another thirty to sixty days before bottling.

7. Bottle-age for one to three months before enjoying.

FRESH FRUIT WINES

20.   Furst raspberry wine

- 3¾ quarts water
- 2¼ lbs. sugar or 2½ lbs. mild honey
- 3-4 lbs. fresh or frozen raspberries
- ½ tsp. acid blend
- 1/8 tsp. tannin
- 1 tsp. yeast nutrient
- 1 Campden tablet, crushed (optional)
- ½ tsp. pectic enzyme
- 1 packet Montrachet or champagne wine yeast

Wash your hands. Put the water mixed with the sugar or honey on the stove to boil. Pick over the berries carefully, discarding any that are not up to par. Rinse lightly. Put the berries into a nylon straining bag and tie the top tightly.

Wash your hands again, rinsing especially well, and put the bag of fruit into the bottom of your primary fermenter and crush the berries within the bag. You can use a sanitized potato masher if you prefer, but hands are the best (besides, they are easy to clean).

Now pour the hot sugar water over the crushed berries. This sets the color. If you prefer, you can chill and reserve half the water beforehand; if you've done so, you can pour it now to bring the temperature down quickly in the primary fermenter. Add the acid, tannin, and yeast nutrient. Cover and fit with an air lock. Wait till the temperature comes down to add the Campden tablet if you use it. Twelve hours after the Campden tablet, add the pectic enzyme. If you don't use the tablet, then merely wait until the must cools down to add the pectic enzyme.

After you add the pectic enzyme, check the PA and write it down. Remember, you can always sweeten later. Put the lid on the primary fermenter and install a rubber bung fitted with an air lock. Make sure the lid is on firmly.

Another twelve hours later, add your yeast simply by sprinkling it on the top of the must (unfermented fruit and sugar water). Don't stir it in. You want the fermentation to start right away. If you scatter the yeast, it will take too long for it to get going.

Once the fermentation gets going, sanitize a large plastic spoon or spatula and carefully stir the contents of the primary fermenter once a day, being careful to maintain the cleanliness of the fermenter lid when you remove and replace it. Be sure the air lock still contains the proper amount of liquid.

After the first excitement of the yeast is over (it takes about one week for all the froth and bubbling to die down to a quiet but obvious activity), remove the bag (don't squeeze). After the sediment has settled down again, check the PA. If it is still above 3 to 4 percent, let the wine ferment for another week, stirring daily, and then rack it into your glass fermenter. Bung and fit with an air lock.

Rack it at least once during secondary fermentation. You don't want any off flavors. Be sure to keep it in a dark jug, or put something over it to keep the light from stealing the color.

In four to six months, check the PA again. Taste the wine. I like it dry, but you might want to sweeten it. Not too much! Add some stabilizer and 2 to 4 ounces of sugar dissolved in water. Bottle, label, let it rest a year, then open and enjoy it. Serve lightly chilled.

OK, so now you get the basic idea. There are a lot of different kinds of fruit out there. Mostly what is going to change is how you process the fruit, the acid content, and the sugar. There are also some small differences in handling the fruit here and there.

21.   Rich apple wine

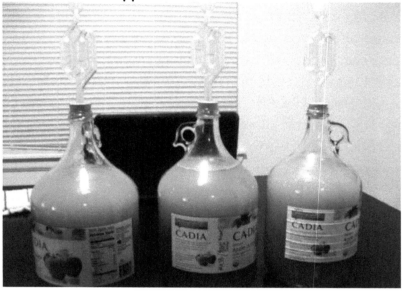

- water to make up the gallon, as needed
- 2 lbs. sugar or 2¼ lbs. mild honey
- 8 lbs. crushed or chopped apples or 24 oz. frozen apple concentrate
- 1 tsp. acid blend (only ½ tsp. if you have tart apples)
- ¼ tsp tannin
- 1 tsp. yeast nutrient
- ½ tsp. pectic enzyme
- 1 Campden tablet, crushed (optional)
- 1 packet champagne wine yeast

Put the water mixed with the sugar or honey on the stove to boil. If you are using crushed or chopped fruit, process it as quickly as possible, stirring in the crushed

Campden tablet. Tart apples mixed with sweeter apples are better than using all sweet dessert apples. Peels are OK, but it's best to get rid of the seeds if you can. Put the crushed or chopped fruit into a nylon straining bag and put it in the bottom of your primary fermenter.

Now pour the hot sugar water over the apples or the frozen apple juice in the primary fermenter. If you prefer, you can chill and reserve half the water beforehand; if you've done so, you can pour it now to bring the temperature down quickly. Add the acid, tannin, and yeast nutrient, but wait till the temperature comes down to add the Campden tablet if you choose to. Cover and fit with an air lock. Twelve hours after the Campden tablet, add the pectic enzyme. If you don't use the tablet, then merely wait until the must cools down to add the pectic enzyme.

Check the PA and write it down.

Twenty-four hours later, add your yeast. Stir daily. After about one week, remove the bag (don't squeeze). After the sediment has settled down again, check the PA. If it is still above 3 to 4 percent PA, let it ferment another week or so, then rack it into your glass fermenter. Bung and fit with an air lock.

Rack the wine at least twice during secondary fermentation.

In four to six months, check the PA to see if it has fermented out. Taste it, too. You might want to sweeten it. Add some stabilizer and 2 to 4 ounces of sugar dissolved in water. Bottle, label, let it rest a year, then open and enjoy it. Serve chilled.

22.   Cider apple wine

- 1 gallon fresh pressed cider or apple juice, no preservatives
- 1 quart water
- 1½ lbs. sugar or 2 lbs. honey
- 1 tsp. acid blend (½ tsp. if apples are tart)
- ¼ tsp. tannin
- 1 tsp. yeast nutrient
- ½ tsp. pectic enzyme
- 1 Campden tablet, crushed (optional)
- 1 packet champagne wine yeast

Put aside 1 quart of the apple juice or cider to drink later. Put the water mixed with the sugar or honey on the stove to boil.

Now pour the hot sugar water over the apple cider. You can do this in a secondary container if you use a funnel and are careful. The cool cider will bring the temperature down quickly. Add the acid, tannin, and yeast nutrient, but wait until the temperature comes down to add the Campden tablet if you choose to. Cover and fit with an air lock. Twelve hours after the Campden tablet, add the pectic enzyme. If you don't use the tablet, then merely wait until the must cools down to add the pectic enzyme.

Check the PA and write it down. It should be within a reasonable range (10 to 13 percent, depending on how sweet the cider was).

Twenty-four hours later, add the yeast. Stir daily for about two weeks. Check the PA. When it is down to 3 to 4 percent, rack the wine into another glass fermenter.

Rack at least twice during secondary fermentation. It might take a while to clear. Keep for at least six months. Serve chilled.

23.   Apricot or peach wine

- 1 gallon water
- 2¼ lbs. sugar or 2½ lbs. mild honey
- 3 lbs. ripe apricots or peaches
- 1½ tsp. acid blend OR juice and zest of 2 lemons
- ¼ tsp. tannin
- 1 tsp. yeast nutrient
- 1 Campden tablet, crushed (optional)
- ½ tsp. pectic enzyme
- 1 packet champagne wine yeast

Put the water mixed with the sugar or honey on the stove to boil. Put the halved fruit into a nylon straining bag and put in the bottom of your primary fermenter. Wash your hands and crush the fruit as much as you can. It will be really gloppy. (Your hands will be gloppy, too. It's good for the complexion.)

Now pour the hot sugar water over the fruit. If you prefer, you can chill and reserve half the water beforehand; if you've done so, you can pour it in now to bring the temperature down quickly. Add the acid, tannin, and yeast nutrient, but wait till the temperature comes down to add the Campden tablet if you choose to. Cover and fit with an air lock. Twelve hours after the Campden tablet, add the pectic enzyme. If you don't use the tablet, then merely wait until the must cools down to add the pectic enzyme.

Check the PA and write it down. It might seem a bit high because of the pulp escaping the nylon bag.

Twenty-four hours later, add the yeast. Stir daily. After about one or two weeks remove the bag (don't squeeze). After the sediment has settled down again, check the PA. If it is above 3 to 4 percent PA, let it go another week or so, then rack it into your glass fermenter. Bung and fit with an air lock. You might have to make up the gallon with a little water to make up for the sediment.

Rack the wine at least twice during secondary fermentation. You don't want any off flavors.

In six months, check the PA to see if it has fermented out. Taste it. You might want to sweeten it. Add some stabilizer and 2 to 4 ounces of sugar dissolved in water. Bottle, label, let it rest a year, then open and enjoy it. Serve chilled.

24. Bodacious banana

- 1 gallon water
- 3 lbs. very ripe (black but not rotten) bananas
- 2 lbs. sugar or 2¼ lbs. mild honey
- 3 tsp. acid blend OR juice of 3 large lemons
- ½ tsp. pectic enzyme
- ¼ tsp. tannin
- 1 tsp. yeast nutrient
- 1 packet champagne wine yeast
- 1 Campden tablet, crushed (optional)

Put half the water on to boil. Wash and slice the bananas, skins and all. Put them in a nylon straining bag and simmer for half an hour in the water. Remove and reserve the nylon straining bag. Pour the liquid into the primary fermenter. Add the straining bag. Boil the sugar or honey with the rest of the water and skim if necessary.

Pour the hot sugar water over the contents of the primary fermenter. Add the acid, tannin, and yeast nutrient, but wait until the temperature comes down to add the Campden tablet if you choose to. Cover and fit with an air lock. Twelve hours after the Campden tablet, add the pectic enzyme. If you don't use the tablet, then merely wait until the must cools down to add the pectic enzyme.

Check the PA and write it down. It might seem a bit high because of the pulp escaping the nylon bag. Don't worry if it looks alarming.

Twenty-four hours later, add the yeast.

Stir daily. Check the PA. (What should it say?) After the froth has died down, you can put it into a secondary fermenter. You might have to top up the gallon with a little water to make up for the sediment. Bung and fit with an air lock.

Rack the wine at least twice during secondary fermentation.

In six months, check the PA to see if it has fermented out. Taste the wine. You might want to sweeten it. Add some stabilizer and 2 to 4 ounces of sugar dissolved in water. Bottle, label, let it rest a year, then open and enjoy it. Serve chilled.

25.   Victory blackberry

- 3¾ quarts water
- 2¼ lbs. sugar or 2½ lbs. mild honey
- 3-4 lbs. fresh or frozen blackberries
- 2 tsp. acid blend
- 1 tsp. yeast nutrient
- 1 Campden tablet, crushed (optional)
- ½ tsp. pectic enzyme
- 1 packet Montrachet yeast

Put the water mixed with the sugar or honey on the stove to boil. Pick over the berries carefully, discarding any that are not up to par. Rinse lightly. Put the berries into a nylon straining bag and tie the top tightly.

Put the bag of fruit into the bottom of your primary fermenter and crush the berries within the bag. You can use a sanitized potato masher if you prefer, but hands are the best. (You might want to wear clean rubber gloves to avoid staining your skin.)

Pour the hot sugar water over the crushed berries. You can chill and reserve half the water beforehand; if you've done so, you can pour it now to bring the temperature down quickly. Add the acid and yeast nutrient, but wait till the temperature comes down to add the Campden tablet if you choose to. Cover and fit with an air lock. Twelve hours after the Campden tablet, add the pectic enzyme. If you don't use the tablet, merely wait until the must cools down to add the pectic enzyme.

Check the PA and write it down.

Twenty-four hours later, add the yeast. Stir daily. After about one week, remove the bag (don't squeeze). After the sediment has settled down again, check the PA. If it is above 3 to 4 percent, give it another week or so, then rack the wine into your glass secondary fermenter. Bung and fit with an air lock.

Rack at least once during secondary fermentation. You don't want any off flavors. Be sure to keep the wine in a dark jug, or to put something over it to keep the light from stealing the color.

In four to six months, check the PA. Taste it, too. I like it dry, but you might want to sweeten it. Not too much! Add some stabilizer and 2 to 4 ounces of sugar dissolved in water. Bottle, label, let it rest a year, then open and enjoy it at room temperature.

26.   Sal's blueberry wine

- 3¾ quarts water
- 2½ lbs. sugar or 3 lbs. mild honey
- 2-3 lbs. fresh or frozen blueberries
- 2 tsp. acid blend
- 1/8 tsp. tannin
- 1 tsp. yeast nutrient
- 1 Campden tablet, crushed (optional)
- ½ tsp. pectic enzyme
- 1 packet Montrachet yeast

Put the water mixed with the sugar or honey on to boil. Pick over the berries carefully. Watch for mold. Discard anything that looks odd. Wash the berries in cool water and drain.

Put the berries in a nylon straining bag and into the primary fermenter, then squish them with your clean hands or a sanitized potato masher. You have to be sure to press them well before you pour the hot water over them. Don't be chagrined by the sickly green color that comes out before you add the hot water. (This makes a good "magic" trick to surprise a child with.) If you cut a fresh blueberry in half with a knife, you'll frequently find that it's green inside. Heat and pressure release the wonderful red/blue that is more familiar.

Pour the hot sugar water over the crushed berries. This sets the color. If you prefer, you can chill and reserve half the water beforehand; if you've done so, you can pour it now to bring the temperature down quickly. Add the acid, tannin, and yeast nutrient, but wait till the temperature comes down to add the Campden tablet if you choose to. Cover and fit with an air lock. Twelve hours after the Campden tablet, add the pectic enzyme. If you don't use the tablet, then merely wait until the must cools down to add the pectic enzyme.

Check the PA and write it down.

Twenty-four hours later, add your yeast. Stir daily. After two weeks, remove the bag (don't squeeze). After the sediment has settled down again, rack the wine into your glass fermenter. Bung and fit with an air lock.

Rack the wine at least once during secondary fermentation. You don't want any off flavors. Be sure to keep it in a dark jug, or put something over it to keep the light from stealing the color.

In four to six months, check the PA. Taste it. When you bottle this one, you might want to sweeten it. Use stabilizer, and add 2-6 ounces of sugar boiled in water. Keep it for a year before drinking, if you can. This is one of those wines that is hard to resist when you want to introduce friends to homemade wines. It has a lovely fragrance and looks like a light red grape wine in the glass. Serve at room temperature or lightly chilled.

In Part Three I'll show you a few ways of dolling this one up. But for now, you might want to add a little more sugar to start with to make a wine that is slightly higher in alcohol, or use another half pound of berries for a richer, stronger wine. Watch the PA so you don't end up with something too sweet.

27.   Denny's pie cherry wine

- 3¾ quarts water
- 2½ lbs. sugar or 3 lbs. mild honey
- 3 lbs. fresh or frozen pie cherries
- 1 tsp. yeast nutrient
- 1/8 tsp. tannin
- 1 Campden tablet, crushed (optional)
- ½ tsp. pectic enzyme
- 1 packet Montrachet yeast

Put the water and sugar or honey on the stove to boil.

Pick over the cherries carefully. Watch for mold. Discard any bad ones. Stem. You don't have to pit these if you are careful not to break the pits when you squish them. Broken pits will make the wine bitter. Cherry pits are very sturdy, though. Wash the cherries in cool water and drain.

Put the cherries in a nylon straining bag and into the primary fermenter, and then squish with your clean hands. They are a firm fruit, so do a good job. Don't they smell wonderful?

Pour the hot sugar water over the crushed cherries. This sets the color. If you prefer, you can chill and reserve half the water beforehand; if you've done so, you can pour it in now to bring the temperature down quickly. Add the yeast nutrient and tannin, but wait till the temperature comes down to add the Campden tablet if you choose to. Cover and fit with an air lock. Twelve hours after the Campden tablet, add the pectic enzyme. If you don't use the tablet, then merely wait until the must cools down to add the pectic enzyme.

Check the PA and write it down.

Twenty-four hours later, add your yeast. Be prepared for a lot of foam. Stir down daily. After two weeks, remove the bag (don't squeeze). After the sediment has settled down again, rack the wine into your glass fermenter. Bung and fit with an air lock.

Rack the wine once or twice during secondary fermentation. Be sure to keep it in a dark jug, or put a piece of cloth around it to keep out light.

In four to six months, check the PA. Taste it. I prefer this wine dry, but you might want to sweeten it. Use stabilizer, and add 2 to 4 ounces of sugar boiled in water. Keep it for a year. Very special! Make as much as you can afford to! Heck, says my partner, make more than you can afford—you won't be sorry! Serve lightly chilled.

28.   Sweet cherry wine

- 3¾ quarts water
- 2 lbs. sugar or 2½ lbs. mild honey
- 4-5 lbs. fresh or frozen sweet cherries
- 2 tsp. acid blend OR juice and zest of 2 lemons
- ¼ tsp. tannin
- 1 tsp. yeast nutrient
- 1 Campden tablet, crushed (optional)
- ½ tsp. pectic enzyme
- 1 packet Montrachet yeast

Put the water and sugar or honey on the stove to boil. Pick over the cherries carefully. Watch for mold. Discard any bad ones. Stem. You don't have to pit these either. Wash the cherries in cool water and drain. If you like, reserve a few of the pits, unbroken, to add to the fruit.

Put the cherries in a nylon straining bag and into the primary fermenter, then squish them with your hands. They are a firm fruit, so do a good job. The color should be great.

Pour the hot sugar water over the crushed cherries. You can chill and reserve half the water beforehand; if you've done so, you can pour it in now to bring the temperature down quickly. Add the acid, tannin, and yeast nutrient, but wait till the temperature comes down to add the Campden tablet if you choose to. Cover and fit with an air lock. Twelve hours after the Campden tablet, add the pectic enzyme. If you don't use the tablet, then merely wait until the must cools down to add the pectic enzyme.

Check the PA and write it down.

Twenty-four hours later, add your yeast. Be prepared for a lot of foam. If it foams up into the air lock, scoop some of the foam out with a sanitized scoop, and clean out the air lock. Stir down daily. After two weeks remove the bag (don't squeeze). After the sediment has settled down again, check the PA. If it is above 3 to 4 percent, let the must ferment for another week or so before racking the wine into your glass fermenter. Bung and fit with an air lock.

Rack the wine once or twice during secondary fermentation. Be sure to keep it in a dark jug, or put a piece of cloth around it to keep out light.

In four to six months, check the PA. Taste it. I prefer this wine dry, but you might want to sweeten it. If so, use stabilizer, and add 2 to 6 ounces of sugar boiled in water. Keep it for a year.

29.   Cheerful cranberry wine

- $3\frac{3}{4}$ quarts water
- 3 lbs. sugar or $3\frac{1}{2}$ lbs. mild honey
- 1 lb. golden raisins (optional)
- $\frac{1}{4}$ tsp. tannin
- $\frac{1}{2}$ tsp. acid blend
- 1 tsp. yeast nutrient
- 1 Campden tablet, crushed (optional)
- $\frac{1}{2}$ tsp. pectic enzyme
- 1 packet Montrachet yeast

Pick over the berries. Discard any bad ones. Put them in some water and bring them just to the boil, then dump them into a nylon straining bag and let them cool down a bit in the primary fermenter.

Put the rest of the water and the sugar or honey on the stove to boil. If you are using the raisins, soak them overnight and chop them up and put them in the bag with the cranberries. Mash the fruit with a sanitized potato masher.

Pour the hot sugar water over the crushed berries. You can chill and reserve half the water beforehand; if you've done so, you can pour it in now to bring the temperature down quickly. Add the tannin, acid blend, and yeast nutrient, but wait till the temperature comes down to add the Campden tablet if you choose to. Cover and fit with an air lock. Twelve hours after the Campden tablet, add the pectic enzyme. If you don't use the tablet, then merely wait until the must cools down to add the pectic enzyme. Be sure to use the pectic enzyme! You don't want cranberry jelly.

Check the PA and write it down.

Twenty-four hours later, add the yeast. Stir down daily. After about one week, remove the bag (don't squeeze). After the sediment has settled down again, check the PA. If it is above 3 to 4 percent, let the must ferment for another week or so before racking the wine into your glass fermenter. Bung and fit with an air lock.

Rack the wine once or twice during secondary fermentation. Be sure to keep it in a dark jug, or put a piece of cloth around it to keep out light.

In four to six months, check the PA. Taste it. I prefer this wine dry, but you might want to sweeten it. Use stabilizer, and add 2 to 6 ounces of sugar boiled in water. Keep it for a year. Serve chilled. Wonderful for the holidays!

30. Currently currant wine

The following recipe is for red and white currants.

- 1 gallon water
- 3 lbs. sugar or 3½ lbs. mild honey
- 3 lbs. ripe currants (don't use more, as they are a high acid fruit)

No acid
- 1/8 tsp. tannin
- ½ tsp. pectic enzyme
- 1 Campden tablet, crushed (optional)
- 1 packet Montrachet yeast

Boil the water and sugar or honey, and skim, if necessary.

Pick over the berries carefully. Discard any bad ones. Put them in a nylon straining bag and crush with clean hands or a sanitized potato masher.

Pour the hot sugar water over the crushed berries. The color should be very pretty if you have used red currants. You can chill and reserve half the water beforehand; if you've done so, you can pour it in now to bring the temperature down quickly. Add the tannin and yeast nutrient, but wait till the temperature comes down to add the Campden tablet if you choose to. Cover and fit with an air lock. Twelve hours after the Campden tablet, add the pectic enzyme. If you don't use the tablet, then merely wait until the must cools down to add the pectic enzyme. Be sure to use the pectic enzyme!

Check the PA and write it down.

Twenty-four hours later, add your yeast. Stir down daily. After one week, remove the bag (don't squeeze). After the sediment has settled down again, check the PA. If it is above 3 to 4 percent, let the must ferment for anther week or so and rack the wine into your glass fermenter.

Rack the wine once or twice during fermentation. Be sure to keep it in a dark jug.

In four to six months, check the PA. Taste it, too. I prefer this wine dry, but you might want to sweeten it. Use stabilizer, and add 2 to 6 ounces of sugar boiled in water. Keep it for a year. The color and flavor should be very nice. Serve lightly chilled. Good with poultry, fish, etc.

31. Black currant wine

- 1 gallon water
- 2½ lbs. sugar or 3 lbs. mild honey
- 2½ lbs. black currants (high acid fruit)
- no acid
- no tannin
- 1 tsp. yeast nutrient
- 1 Campden tablet, crushed (optional)
- ½ tsp. pectic enzyme
- 1 packet Montrachet yeast

Boil the water and sugar or honey, and skim, if necessary.

Pick over the berries carefully. Discard any bad ones. Put them in a nylon straining bag and crush with clean hands or a sanitized potato masher. Black currants will stain.

Pour the hot sugar water over the crushed berries. If you prefer, you can chill and reserve half the water beforehand; if you've done so, you can pour it in now to bring the temperature down quickly. Add the yeast nutrient, but wait till the temperature comes down to add the Campden tablet if you choose to. Cover and fit with an air lock. Twelve hours after the Campden tablet, add the pectic enzyme. If you don't use the tablet, merely wait until the must cools down to add the pectic enzyme. Be sure to use the pectic enzyme!

Check the PA and write it down.

Twenty-four hours later, add your yeast. Stir down daily. After the first excitement of the yeast is over (about one week), remove the bag (don't squeeze). After the sediment has settled down again, check the PA. If it is above 3 to 4 percent, let the must ferment for another week or so and rack the wine into your glass fermenter. Bung and fit with an air lock.

Rack the wine once or twice during secondary fermentation. Be sure to keep it in a dark jug, or put a piece of cloth around it to keep out the light.

In four to six months, check the PA. Taste it, too. I prefer this wine dry, but you might want to sweeten it. It's very fragrant. Use stabilizer, and add 2 to 6 ounces of sugar boiled in water. Keep it for a year. Serve lightly chilled.

32. Elderberry wine

- 1 gallon water
- 2½ lbs. sugar or 3 lbs. mild honey
- 3 lbs. ripe elderberries
- 2 tsp. acid blend
- 1 tsp. yeast nutrient
- 1 Campden tablet, crushed (optional)
- ½ tsp. pectic enzyme

no tannin

- 1 packet Montrachet yeast

Put the water and sugar or honey on the stove to boil. Pick over the berries carefully. Take them off the stems. Discard any bad ones. Put them in a nylon straining bag and crush them with clean hands in sanitized rubber gloves or with a sanitized potato masher. They stain like all get out.

Now pour the hot sugar water over the crushed berries. If you prefer, you can chill and reserve half the water beforehand; if you've done so, you can pour it in now to bring the temperature down quickly. Add the acid and yeast nutrient, but wait until the temperature comes down before adding the Campden tablet if you choose to. Cover and fit with an airlock. Twelve hours after the Campden tablet, add the pectic enzyme. If you don't use the tablet, then merely wait until the must cools down to add the pectic enzyme. Be sure to use the pectic enzyme.

Check the PA and write it down.

Twenty-four hours later, add the yeast. Stir down daily. This can froth quite a bit. After two weeks, remove the bag (don't squeeze). After the sediment has settled down again, check the PA. If it is above 3 to 4 percent, let the must ferment for another week or so and then rack the wine into your glass fermenter. Bung and fit with an air lock.

Rack the wine once or twice during secondary fermentation. Be sure to keep it in a dark jug, or put a piece of cloth around it to keep out the light.

In four to six months, check the PA. Taste it, too. I prefer this wine dry, but you might want to sweeten it. Use stabilizer, and add 2 to 6 ounces of sugar boiled in water. Keep it for a year. Isn't that a lovely color? Serve at room temperature.

33.   Gooseberry wine

- 1 gallon water
- 2½ lbs. sugar or 3 lbs. mild honey
- 3 lbs. gooseberries (high acid fruit)
- no acid blend
- no tannin
- 1 tsp. yeast nutrient
- 1 Campden tablet, crushed (optional)
- ½ tsp. pectic enzyme
- 1 packet champagne yeast

Boil the water and sugar or honey, and skim, if necessary. Pick over the berries carefully. Take off the stems. You can leave the tails. Discard any bad berries. Put them in a nylon straining bag and crush them with clean hands or a sanitized potato masher.

Pour the hot sugar water over the crushed berries. If you prefer, you can chill and reserve half the water beforehand; if you've done so, you can pour it in now to bring the temperature down quickly. Add the yeast nutrient, but wait until the temperature comes down to add the Campden tablet if you choose to. Cover and fit with an air lock. Twelve hours after the Campden tablet, add the pectic enzyme. If you don't use the tablet, then merely wait until the must cools down to add the pectic enzyme. Be sure to use the pectic enzyme!

Check the PA and write it down.

Twenty-four hours later, add your yeast. Stir down daily. After about one week, remove the bag (don't squeeze). After the sediment has settled down again, check the PA. If it is above 3 to 4 percent, let the must ferment for another week or so and then rack the wine into your glass fermenter. Bung and fit with an air lock.

Rack the wine once or twice during secondary fermentation.

In four to six months, check the PA. Taste it, too. I prefer this wine dry, but you might want to sweeten it. Use stabilizer, and add 2 to 6 ounces of sugar boiled in water. Keep it for a year. Excellent with poultry, fish, and grain dishes. Serve chilled.

34.   Grapefruit wine

- $3\frac{3}{4}$ quarts water
- 2 lbs. sugar or $2\frac{1}{4}$ lbs. light honey (clover is good)
- 6 big juicy grapefruit, pink or white
- 1 12 oz. can frozen white grape juice or 1 lb. golden raisins or 1 pint white grape concentrate from wine supply store
- no acid
- 1 tsp. yeast nutrient
- $\frac{1}{4}$ tsp. tannin
- 1 Campden tablet, crushed (optional)
- $\frac{1}{2}$ tsp. pectic enzyme
- 1 packet champagne yeast

Boil the water and sugar or honey, and skim, if necessary.

Prepare the zest of two or three of the grapefruits. Then peel the grapefruits and section them, getting rid of as much white pith as you can. Put the segments and the zest (and soaked, cut-up raisins, if you use them) in a nylon straining bag, and put it in the bottom of a primary fermenter. Mash with very clean hands or a sanitized potato masher.

If you aren't using raisins, add the grape juice or grape concentrate now. Pour the hot sugar water over the crushed fruit. If you prefer, you can chill and reserve half the water beforehand; if you've done so, you can pour it in now to bring the temperature down quickly. Add the yeast nutrient and tannin, but wait till the temperature comes down to add the Campden tablet if you choose to. Cover and fit with an air lock. Twelve hours after the Campden tablet, add the pectic enzyme. If you don't use the tablet, then merely wait until the must cools down to add the pectic enzyme. Be sure to use the pectic enzyme.

Check the PA and write it down.

Twenty-four hours later, add your yeast. Stir down daily. After about one week, remove the bag (don't squeeze). After the sediment has settled down again, check the PA. If it is above 3 to 4 percent, let the must ferment for another week or so, and rack the wine into your glass fermenter.

Rack the wine once or twice during fermentation.

In four to six months, check the PA. Taste it. You might want to sweeten it. Use stabilizer, and add 2 to 6 ounces of sugar boiled in water. Keep it for six months to a year before drinking. Serve chilled, maybe even with ice. It should have a light, pleasant fragrance.

Wine grape white wine

Equipment:
- a BIG nylon bag AND an extra primary fermenter
- 16-18 lbs. wine grapes
- 1 Campden tablet, crushed (highly recommended)
- 1 packet champagne or Montrachet yeast
- Check over the grapes, get rid of any moldy ones, get rid of stems, leaves, bugs, stray satyrs and their panpipes, etc.

Put the grapes into a nylon straining bag (or two, if you can't get a really big one), and crush the grapes into the bottom of the extra primary fermenter. Use very clean hands, or a big sanitized potato masher. Squish the daylights out of the grapes, turning the bag or bags around and around. (If you have a grape crusher, or can borrow one, use it, of course.) Add the Campden tablet now. You should have juice up to the one-gallon mark and somewhat over, because of the fruit pulp.

Pour out the grape juice into the second primary fermenter and squeeze or press the remaining pulp as best you can (a grape press would be nice, but not too many people have one lying around).

Let the juice settle out a bit and check the PA of a clear sample. You are aiming for 10 to 12 percent PA. If it is less than that, then your grapes weren't as sweet as they should have been. You'll have to add some sugar dissolved in a little water to make it up.

If it's more than that, it's OK, up to 13 percent. If it is more than THAT, take some juice out and add water to make it up and thin out the sugar from the grapes.

If you know how to use an acid test kit, then check the acid and adjust that, too, to 70 percent. If you don't, then don't worry about it. Everything is probably OK.

Cover for 12 hours and fit with an air lock. Add the yeast. After fermentation starts, stir daily. When the PA gets down to about 4 percent, let the juice settle. It might be pinkish, but that's OK. Many white wines are.

Rack the wine off into a secondary glass container, topping up with a little water or fresh juice if necessary. After another four weeks, check the PA and rack off into a clean secondary fermenter. Bung and fit with an air lock.

36.   Dragon lady wild grape wine

- 1 gallon water
- 2½ lbs. sugar or 3 lbs. mild honey
- 3 lbs. wild or other grapes
- 1 tsp. acid blend
- ¼ tsp. tannin
- 1 tsp. yeast nutrient
- 1 Campden tablet, crushed (highly recommended)
- ½ tsp. pectic enzyme
- 1 packet Montrachet yeast

Boil the water and sugar or honey, and skim, if necessary. Pick over the grapes carefully. Take them off the stems. Discard any bad ones. Put them in a nylon straining bag and crush with clean hands or a potato masher. They stain like all get out.

Pour the hot sugar water over the crushed grapes. If you prefer, you can chill and reserve half the water beforehand; if you've done so, you can pour it in now to bring the temperature down quickly. Add the acid, tannin, and yeast nutrient, but wait till the temperature comes down to add the Campden tablet and the pectic enzyme. Be sure to use the pectic enzyme. Cover and fit with an air lock.

Check the PA and write it down.

Twenty-four hours later, add your yeast. Stir down daily. After the first excitement of the yeast is over (about one week), remove the bag (don't squeeze). After the sediment has settled down again, check the PA. If it is above 3 to 4 percent, let the must ferment for another week or so, remove the bag, and rack the wine into your glass fermenter.

Rack the wine once or twice during secondary fermentation. Bung and fit with an air lock. Be sure to keep it in a dark jug, or put a piece of cloth around it to keep out the light.

In four to six months, check the PA. Taste it. I prefer this wine bone dry, but you might want to sweeten it when you bottle it. Use stabilizer, and add 2 to 6 ounces of sugar boiled in water. Keep it for a year. If you get a dark stain on the sides of the bottle, don't worry—it's the nature of some dark fruits with lots of color. Serve at room temperature if red, and chilled if white.

37.   Kiwi wine

- 3¾ quarts water
- 2¼ lbs. sugar or 2½ lbs. mild honey
- 3 lbs. fresh kiwifruit
- 1 tsp. acid blend OR juice and zest of one small lemon
- 1/8 tsp. tannin
- 1 Campden tablet, crushed (optional)
- 1 tsp. yeast nutrient
- ½ tsp. pectic enzyme
- 1 packet champagne wine yeast

Put the water mixed with the sugar or honey on the stove to boil. Peel and chop the kiwifruit, put it into a nylon straining bag, and tie the top tightly. Put the bag of fruit into the bottom of your primary fermenter, and use your clean hands or a sanitized potato masher to crush the fruit.

Pour the hot sugar water over the crushed fruit. If you prefer, you can chill and reserve half the water beforehand; if you've done so, you can pour it in now to bring the temperature down quickly. Add the acid, tannin, and yeast nutrient, but wait till the temperature comes down to add the Campden tablet if you choose to. Cover and fit with an air lock. Twelve hours after the Campden tablet, add the pectic enzyme. If you don't use the tablet, then merely wait until the must cools down to add the pectic enzyme.

Check the PA and write it down.

Twenty-four hours later, add the yeast. You want the fermentation to start right away. Stir daily.

After about one week remove the bag (don't squeeze). After the sediment has settled down again, check the PA. If it is above 3 to 4 percent, give it another week or so, and rack the wine into your glass secondary fermenter. Bung and fit with an air lock.

Rack the wine at least once during fermentation.

In four to six months, check the PA. Taste it, too. You might want to sweeten it. Add some stabilizer and 2 to 4 ounces of sugar dissolved in water. Bottle it, label it, let it rest six months, then open and enjoy it. A nice table wine, served lightly chilled.

38.   Meg's melon wine

- 3½ quarts or so of water
- 2 lbs. of sugar or 2 lbs. light honey (highly recommended)
- 3-4 lbs. very ripe melon from the centers of the melons
- 2 tsp. acid blend
- 1 tsp. yeast nutrient
- 1 Campden tablet, crushed (optional)
- 1 packet champagne yeast

Boil the water and sugar or honey, and skim, if necessary. Cut the melon in chunks and put them in a fine nylon straining bag and into the bottom of a primary fermenter. With clean hands or a sanitized potato masher, squish the melon. Don't worry about seeds.

Pour the hot sugar water over the crushed fruit. If you prefer, you can chill and reserve half the water beforehand; if you've done so, you can pour it in now to bring the temperature down quickly. Add the acid, tannin, and yeast nutrient, but wait till the temperature comes down to add the Campden tablet if you choose to. Cover and fit with an air lock. Twelve hours after the Campden tablet, add the pectic enzyme. If you don't use the tablet, then merely wait until the must cools down to add the pectic enzyme.

After a week, lift out what remains of the melon, and let the bag drain into the primary fermenter. Don't squeeze. When the wine settles, check the PA. If it is above 3 to 4 percent, let it continue for another week or so, then rack the wine off into a glass secondary fermenter. Bung and fit with an air lock. A couple of weeks after that, do it again, making up the level with a little boiled water if you have to.

Rack the wine again in the next two to six months, and wait for it to ferment out and clear. This is better when sweetened a little, so stabilize, and add 2 to 6 ounces of sugar in a bit of water, and bottle. Keep it six months to a year. Serve chilled.

39. Mulberry revenge

- 3¾ quarts water
- 2¼ lbs. sugar or 2½ lbs. mild honey
- 3-4 lbs. fresh or frozen mulberries
- 1 tsp. acid blend OR juice and zest of one small lemon
- 1/8 tsp. tannin
- 1 tsp. yeast nutrient
- 1 Campden tablet, crushed (optional)
- ½ tsp. pectic enzyme
- 1 packet Montrachet or champagne wine yeast

Put the water mixed with the sugar or honey on the stove to boil. Pick over the berries carefully, discarding any that are not up to par. Rinse lightly. Put the berries into a nylon straining bag and tie the top tightly.

Put the bag of fruit into the bottom of your primary fermenter and crush the berries within the bag. You can use a sanitized potato masher if you prefer, but hands in sanitized rubber gloves are best.

Pour the hot sugar water over the crushed berries. You can chill and reserve half the water beforehand; if you've done so, you can pour it in now to bring the temperature down quickly. Add the acid, tannin, and yeast nutrient, but wait till the temperature comes down to add the Campden tablet if you choose to. Cover and fit with an air lock. Twelve hours after the Campden tablet, add the pectic enzyme. If you don't use the tablet, merely wait until the must cools down to add the pectic enzyme.

Check the PA and write it down.

Twenty-four hours later, add the yeast. Stir daily. After two weeks, remove the bag (don't squeeze). After the sediment has settled down again, check the PA. If it is above 3 to 4 percent, give it another week or so, and rack the wine into your glass secondary fermenter. Bung and fit with an air lock.

Rack the wine at least once during fermentation. Be sure to keep it in a dark jug, or put something over it to keep the light from stealing the color.

In four to six months, check the PA. Taste it, too. I like it dry, but you might want to sweeten it. Add some stabilizer and 2 to 4 ounces of sugar dissolved in water. Bottle it, label it, let it rest a year, then open and enjoy it. A nice table wine, served lightly chilled. It's a good one on which to start people new to fruit wines.

40.   Orange wine

- 3¾ quarts water
- 2 lbs. sugar or 2¼ lbs. light honey (orange blossom is good!)
- 10 heavy juice oranges

No acid
- ¼ tsp. tannin
- 1 tsp. yeast nutrient
- 1 Campden tablet, crushed (optional)
- ½ tsp. pectic enzyme
- 1 packet champagne yeast

Boil the water and sugar or honey, and skim, if necessary. Use the zest of four or five of the oranges. Then peel the fruits, and section them, getting rid of as much white pith as you can. Put the segments and the zest in a nylon straining bag, and put it in the bottom of a primary fermenter. Mash with very clean hands or a sanitized potato masher.

Pour the hot sugar water over the crushed fruit. If you prefer, you can chill and reserve half the water beforehand; if you've done so, you can pour it in now to bring the temperature down quickly. Add the yeast nutrient and tannin, but wait till the temperature comes down to add the Campden tablet if you choose to. Cover and fit with an air lock. Twelve hours after the Campden tablet, add the pectic enzyme. If you don't use the tablet, merely wait until the must cools down to add the pectic enzyme. Be sure to use the pectic enzyme.

Check the PA and write it down.

Twenty-four hours later, add the yeast. Stir down daily. After about one week, remove the bag (don't squeeze). After the sediment has settled down again, check the PA. If it is above 3 to 4 percent, let the must ferment for another week or so and rack the wine into your glass fermenter. Bung and fit with an air lock.

41.   Matched pear

- 3½ quarts or so of water
- 2 lbs. of sugar or 2 lbs. light honey (highly recommended)
- 4 lbs. ripe pears
- 1 Campden tablet, crushed (recommended)
- 2 tsp. acid blend
- 1 tsp. yeast nutrient
- ¼ tsp. tannin
- ½ tsp. pectic enzyme
- 1 packet champagne yeast

Boil the water and sugar or honey, and skim, if necessary. Wash the pears well, remove the stems, cut them in half, and take out the cores. No need to peel. Cut the pears in chunks and put them in a fine nylon straining bag and into the bottom of a primary fermenter. With a sanitized potato masher, mash the pears with the Campden tablet.

Pour the hot sugar water over the crushed fruit. If you prefer, you can chill and reserve half the water beforehand; if you've done so, you can pour it in now to bring the temperature down quickly. Add the yeast nutrient and tannin, but wait till the temperature comes down to add another Campden tablet if you choose to. Cover and fit with an air lock. Twelve hours after the Campden tablet, add the pectic enzyme. If you don't use the tablet, merely wait until the must cools down to add the pectic enzyme. Be sure to use the pectic enzyme. Stir daily.

After a week, lift out the pear pulp, and let the bag drain into the primary fermenter. When the wine settles, check the PA. If it is above 3 to 4 percent, let it continue for another week or so, then rack the wine off into a glass secondary fermenter. Bung and fit with an air lock. A couple of weeks after that, do it again, making up the level with a little boiled water if you have to.

Rack the wine again in the next two to six months, and wait for it to ferment out and clear. Bottle the wine. This is better when sweetened a little, so stabilize it, and add 2 to 6 ounces of sugar in a bit of water, if you like. Keep six months to a year. Serve chilled.

42. **Hawaiian pineapple wine**

- 3½ quarts or so of water
- 2 lbs. of sugar or 2 lbs. light honey (highly recommended)
- 3-4 lbs. ripe pineapples
- ½ tsp. acid blend
- ¼ tsp. tannin
- 1 tsp. yeast nutrient
- 1 Campden tablet, crushed (recommended)
- ½ tsp. pectic enzyme
- 1 packet champagne yeast

Boil most of the water and all the sugar or honey, and skim, if necessary.

Remove the leaves and skin the pineapple, saving any juice you lose. Watch out for stickers! Don't worry if you don't get all the knots out of the skin. Cut the pineapple in half, and take out the core, then cut the fruit into small pieces over a bowl, saving the juice. Put it in a nylon straining bag and into the bottom of a primary fermenter. With a sanitized potato masher, mash the pineapple with the Campden tablet.

Pour the sugar water over the fruit. See if you need to add the rest of the water to make up the gallon, allowing for the bulk of the fruit, of course. When cooled, add acid, tannin, yeast nutrient, and another Campden tablet if you choose to. Cover and fit with an air lock. Twelve hours after the Campden tablet, add the pectic enzyme. If you don't use the tablet, merely wait until the must cools down to add the pectic enzyme.

Twenty-four hours later add the yeast. Stir daily.

After a week, lift out what remains of the pineapples, and let the bag drain into the primary fermenter (don't squeeze). When the wine settles, check the PA. If it is above 3 to 4 percent, let it continue for another week or so, then rack the wine off into a glass secondary fermenter. Bung and fit with an air lock. A couple of weeks after that, do it again, making up the level with a little boiled water if you have to.

Rack the wine again in the next two to six months, and wait for it to ferment out and clear. Pineapple wine is better when sweetened a little, so stabilize it, and add 2 to 6 ounces of sugar in a bit of water, and bottle. It should be very fragrant. Keep six months to a year. Serve chilled

43.   Plum or nectarine wine

- 3½ quarts or so of water
- 2 lbs. of sugar or 2 lbs. light honey (highly recommended)
- 4 lbs. ripe sweet plums or nectarines or 3 lbs. wild plums
- 1½ tsp. acid blend (none for wild plums)
- 1/8 tsp. tannin
- 1 tsp. yeast nutrient
- 1 Campden tablet, crushed (recommended)
- ½ tsp. pectic enzyme
- 1 packet champagne or Montrachet yeast

Boil most of the water and all of the sugar or honey, and skim, if necessary.

Wash, stem, and pit the plums. No need to peel them. Then cut them into small pieces over a bowl, saving the juice. Put it in a nylon straining bag and into the bottom of a primary fermenter. With a sanitized potato masher, mash the fruit.

Pour the water and sugar over the fruit. See if you need to add the rest of the water to make up the gallon, allowing for the bulk of the fruit, of course. When cooled, add acid, tannin, yeast nutrient, and the Campden tablet if you choose to. Cover and fit with an air lock. Twelve hours after the Campden tablet, add the pectic enzyme. If you don't use the tablet, merely wait until the must cools down to add the pectic enzyme.

Twenty-four hours later, add the yeast. Stir daily.

After a week, lift out what remains of the fruit, and let the bag drain. When the wine settles, check the PA. If it is above 3 to 4 percent, let it continue for another week or so, then rack the wine off into a glass secondary fermenter. Bung and fit with an air lock. A couple of weeks after that, do it again, making up the level with a little boiled water if you have to.

Rack the wine again in the next two to six months, and wait for it to ferment out and clear. Plum wine is better when sweetened a little, so stabilize it, and add 2-6 ounces of sugar in a bit of water, and bottle. Keep it six months to a year. Serve chilled.

44.   Rhubarb Wine

- 1 gallon water
- 2½ lbs. of sugar or 3 lbs. light honey (highly recommended)
- 3 lbs. rhubarb stalks, the redder the better, fresh or frozen
- 1 6 oz. can frozen apple or white grape juice, optional
- no acid blend
- 1/8 tsp. tannin
- 1 tsp. yeast nutrient
- 1 Campden tablet, crushed (optional)
- ½ tsp. pectic enzyme
- 1 packet champagne or Montrachet yeast

Boil the water and sugar or honey, and skim, if necessary. Wash and cut the rhubarb stalks into small pieces. Put them in a nylon straining bag and into the bottom of a primary fermenter. With a sanitized potato masher, mash the fruit.

If you use the apple juice or white grape juice, leave out ¼ lb. sugar or honey. Pour the hot water and sugar over the fruit. Let it cool a bit, then mash it again, and add the apple or grape juice if you are using them. When cooled, add the tannin, yeast nutrient, and the Campden tablet if you choose to. Cover and fit with an air lock. Twelve hours after the Campden tablet, add the pectic enzyme. If you don't use the tablet, merely wait until the must cools down to add the pectic enzyme.

Twenty-four hours later, add the yeast. Stir daily.

After three to four days, lift out what remains of the fruit, and let the bag drain. Don't squeeze. When the wine settles, check the PA. If it is above 3 to 4 percent, let it continue for another week or so, then rack the wine off into a glass secondary fermenter with a little boiled water if you have to. Bung and fit with an air lock.

Rack the wine again in the next two to six months, and wait for it to ferment out and clear. Rhubarb wine is good dry, but you might like it better sweetened a little. If so, stabilize it, add 2 to 4 ounces of sugar in a bit of water, and bottle it. Keep it six months to a year. Serve chilled. Very nice with poultry, fish, and grain dishes.

45.   Lips like strawberry wine

- 3½ quarts or so of water
- 2 lbs. of sugar or 2 lbs. light honey (highly recommended)
- 4 lbs. ripe sweet strawberries, fresh or frozen
- 1 tsp. acid blend OR juice of one large lemon
- 1/8 tsp. tannin
- 1 tsp. yeast nutrient
- 1 Campden tablet, crushed (optional)
- ½ tsp. pectic enzyme
- 1 packet champagne or Montrachet yeast

Boil most of the water and all of the sugar or honey, and skim, if necessary.

Wash and stem the berries. Pick them over and cut out any bad parts. Put them in a nylon straining bag and into the bottom of a primary fermenter. Squash the strawberries with your clean hands or a sanitized potato masher. You'll get a frothy pink substance.

Pour the hot water and sugar over the fruit. See if you need to add the rest of the water to make up the gallon, allowing for the bulk of the fruit, of course. When cooled, add acid, tannin yeast nutrient, and the Campden tablet if you choose to. Cover and fit with an air lock. Twelve hours after the Campden tablet, add the pectic enzyme. If you don't use the tablet, merely wait until the must cools down to add the pectic enzyme.

Twenty-four hours later, add the yeast. Stir daily.

After a week, lift out what remains of the fruit, and let the bag drain. Do not squeeze the bag. When the wine settles, check the PA. If it is above 3 to 4 percent, let it continue for another week or so, then rack the wine off into a glass secondary fermenter, with a little boiled water if you have to. Bung and fit with an air lock.

Rack the wine again in the next two to six months, and wait for it to ferment out and clear. I like strawberry wine very dry. If you would prefer it sweetened a little, then stabilize it, add 2 to 6 ounces of sugar in a bit of water, and bottle it. Keep it six months to a year. Serve chilled. Excellent for Saint Valentine's Day.

46.   Tomato wine

- 3½ quarts or so of water
- 2 lbs. of sugar or 2 lbs. light honey
- 4 lbs. ripe tomatoes, red or yellow
- 2 tsp. acid blend
- 1/8 tsp. tannin
- 1 tsp. yeast nutrient
- 1 Campden tablet, crushed (optional)
- ½ tsp. pectic enzyme
- 1 packet champagne or Montrachet yeast

Boil most of the water and all of the sugar or honey, and skim, if necessary.

Wash the fruit. Look the tomatoes over and cut out any bad parts as you cut them into chunks over a bowl. Put them in a nylon straining bag and into the bottom of a primary fermenter with any juice caught in the bowl. Squash the fruit with your clean hands or a sanitized potato masher.

Pour the hot water and sugar over the fruit. See if you need to add the rest of the water to make up the gallon, allowing for the bulk of the tomatoes, of course. When cooled, add acid, tannin, yeast nutrient, and the Campden tablet if you choose to. Cover and fit with an air lock. Twelve hours after the Campden tablet, add the pectic enzyme. If you don't use the tablet, merely wait until the must cools down to add the pectic enzyme.

Twenty-four hours later, add the yeast. Stir daily.

After a week, remove what remains of the fruit, and let the bag drain into the primary fermenter. Don't squeeze. When the wine settles, check the PA. If it is above 3 to 4 percent, let it continue for another week or so, then rack the wine off into a glass secondary fermenter, with a little boiled water if you have to.

Rack the wine again in the next two to six months, and wait for it to ferment out and clear. The color of the wine varies from a red gold to gold. Tomato wine is better when sweetened a little, so stabilize it and add 2 to 4 ounces of sugar in a bit of water, and bottle. Keep six months to a year. Serve chilled.

CANNED FRUITS WINES

47.   Peachy can dew wine

- water, about $3\frac{1}{2}$ quarts
- 2 16 oz. (or so) cans of peach slices or halves in light syrup
- 2 lbs. sugar (if fruit is canned in its own or something else's juices, add about another $\frac{1}{4}$-$\frac{1}{2}$ lb. of sugar)
- 1 cup fresh squeezed or frozen orange juice (optional)
- 2 tsps. acid blend
- 1 tsp. yeast nutrient
- $\frac{1}{4}$ tsp. tannin
- 1 Campden tablet, crushed (optional)
- $\frac{1}{2}$ tsp. pectic enzyme
- 1 packet champagne yeast

Heat the water. Drain the syrup from the fruit. Place the fruit into a nylon straining bag and put it in the bottom of a sanitized primary fermenter. Add the orange juice if you wish. It helps perk up the taste.

Measure out 3½ quarts of warm water to start with, and add the fruit syrup. Add 1½ pounds of the sugar and stir until dissolved. Be sure it is dissolved. Check the PA. For this wine you want about 12 percent potential alcohol.

You can never tell about fruit syrups. Supposedly there are standards as to how much sugar is in them, but with fruit solids and volume and all that, it's best to check.

If the PA is below 12 percent (and it probably will be), stir in the other half pound of sugar. Stir it in well and check the PA again. Don't worry if it is a degree off. This is art, not science. You could go up to 14 percent and a little beyond if you wanted to, but this is best as a medium sort of wine. The fruit still has sugar in it, too, don't forget.

Pour the water and sugar/syrup mixture over the fruit, and add the acid, yeast nutrient, and tannin. If you don't have a little over a gallon of must in the fermenter, add another couple of cups of water and check the PA again.

After the mixture cools down, add a crushed Campden tablet, if you choose to use one. Cover and fit with an air lock. Twelve hours after the Campden tablet, add the pectic enzyme. If you don't use the tablet, merely wait until the must cools down to add the pectic enzyme.

Twenty-four hours later, add the yeast.

Let ferment for five days, stirring daily. When the PA falls to 3 to 4 percent, remove the fruit. Drain it well, but don't squeeze; it will simply turn to fine pulp that will end up displacing the wine. Let the wine settle, then rack into a gallon jug. Bung and fit with an air lock.

Rack the wine once or twice over the next three to six months. Sometimes this ferments out quite quickly, depending on the weather and the reaction of the yeast and fruit.

When the fermentation is done, taste the wine and decide how you like it. If you've gotten good canned peaches, it should taste pretty good, though you'll probably be able to tell that it needs to sit in the bottle for a while. If the peaches weren't the best, it might taste rather harsh. Fear not. Add stabilizer, sweeten it up a bit with a couple of ounces of dissolved sugar or boiled honey, and sit back and let the bottle and time do their magic.

48.   Canned blueberry wine

- water, about 3½ quarts
- 2 16 oz. (or so) cans of blueberries or blackberries in light syrup
- 2 lbs. sugar (if fruit is canned in heavy syrup, subtract another ¼ lb. of sugar)
- 2 tsp. acid blend OR zest and juice of 2 large lemons
- 1/8 tsp. tannin
- 1 tsp. yeast nutrient
- 1 Campden tablet, crushed (optional)
- ½ tsp. pectic enzyme
- 1 packet Montrachet yeast

Heat the water. Drain the syrup from the fruit. Place the fruit (and zest if you are using it) into a nylon straining bag and put it in the bottom of a sanitized primary fermenter.

Measure out 3½ quarts of warm water to start with and add the fruit syrup. Add 1½ pounds of the sugar and stir till dissolved. Be sure it is dissolved. Check the PA. For this wine you want about 12 percent potential alcohol.

If the PA is below 12 percent (and it probably will be), stir in the other one half pound of sugar well and check the PA again. Don't worry if it is a degree off. The fruit still has sugar in it, too, don't forget.

Pour the water/sugar/syrup mixture over the fruit and add the acid, yeast nutrient, tannin, and lemon juice if you are using it instead of the acid. After the must cools, add a crushed Campden tablet, if you choose to use one. Cover and fit with an air lock. Twelve hours after the Campden tablet, add the pectic enzyme. If you don't use the tablet, merely wait until the must cools down to add the pectic enzyme.

Twenty-four hours later, add the yeast.

Let the wine ferment for five days, stirring daily. When the PA falls to 3 to 4 percent, remove the fruit. Drain it well, but don't squeeze; it will turn to fine pulp that will displace the wine. Let the wine settle, then rack it into a gallon jug. Bung and fit with an air lock.

Rack the wine once or twice more over the next three to six months. When the fermentation is done, taste it and decide how you like it. If you want it sweeter, stabilize it and sweeten it up a bit with a couple of ounces of dissolved sugar or boiled honey, and bottle it.

49.   Canned pie cherry wine

- water, about $3\frac{1}{2}$ quarts
- 2 16 oz. (or so) cans pie cherries in light syrup
- 2 lbs. sugar (if fruit is canned in heavy syrup, subtract another $\frac{1}{4}$ lb. of sugar; if in water, add $\frac{1}{4}$ lb.)
- 1 tsp. acid blend
- 1 tsp. yeast nutrient
- 1 Campden tablet, crushed (optional)
- $\frac{1}{2}$ tsp. pectic enzyme
- 1 packet Montrachet yeast

Heat the water. Drain the syrup from the fruit. Place the fruit into a nylon straining bag and put it in the bottom of a sanitized primary fermenter.

Measure out $3\frac{1}{4}$ quarts of warm water to start with, and add the fruit syrup. Add $1\frac{1}{2}$ pounds of the sugar and stir till dissolved. Be sure it is dissolved. Check the PA.

For this wine you want about 12 percent potential alcohol.

If the PA is below 12 percent (and it probably will be), stir in the other half pound of sugar well and check the PA again. Don't worry if it is a degree off. The fruit still has sugar in it, too, don't forget.

Pour the water and sugar syrup mixture over the fruit, and add the acid, yeast nutrient, and tannin. After the must cools, add a crushed Campden tablet, if you choose to use one. Cover and fit with an air lock. Twelve hours after the Campden tablet, add the pectic enzyme. If you don't use the tablet, merely wait until the must cools down to add the pectic enzyme.

Twenty-four hours later, add the yeast.

Let it ferment for five days, stirring daily. When the PA falls to 3 to 4 percent, remove the fruit. Drain it well, but don't squeeze; it will simply turn to fine pulp that will displace the wine. Let the wine settle, then rack it into a gallon jug. Bung and fit with an air lock.

Rack the wine once or twice over the next three to six months. When the fermentation is done, taste and decide how you like it. If you want it sweeter, stabilize it, and sweeten it up a bit with a couple of ounces of dissolved sugar or boiled honey, and bottle it.

Canned pineapple wine

- water, about $3\frac{1}{2}$ quarts
- 2 16 oz. (or so) cans of pineapple, crushed in juice
- 2 lbs. sugar (if fruit is canned in syrup, subtract another $\frac{1}{4}$ lb. of sugar) or 2 lbs. light honey
- 1 tsp. acid blend
- 1 tsp. yeast nutrient
- 1 Campden tablet, crushed (optional)
- $\frac{1}{2}$ tsp. pectic enzyme
- 1 packet champagne yeast

Heat the water. Drain the juice from the fruit, place the fruit into a nylon straining bag, and put it in the bottom of a sanitized primary fermenter. (The fruit is already crushed.)

Measure out $3\frac{1}{2}$ quarts of warm water to start with, and add the fruit juice. Add $1\frac{1}{2}$ pounds of the sugar and stir till dissolved. Be sure it is dissolved. Check the PA.

For this wine you want about 12 percent potential alcohol.

If the PA is below 12 percent (and it probably will be), stir in the other ½ pound of sugar well and check the PA again. Don't worry if it is a degree off.

Pour the water and sugar syrup mixture over the fruit in the fermenter and add the acid, yeast nutrient, and tannin. After the must cools, add a crushed Campden tablet, if you choose to use one. Cover and fit with an air lock. Twelve hours after the Campden tablet, add the pectic enzyme. If you don't use the tablet, merely wait until the must cools down to add the pectic enzyme.

Twenty-four hours later, add the yeast.

Let it ferment for five days, stirring daily. When the PA falls to 3 to 4 percent, remove the fruit. Drain it well, but don't squeeze; it will simply turn to fine pulp that will displace the wine. Let the wine settle, then rack it into a gallon jug. Bung and fit with an air lock.

Rack the wine once or twice over the next three to six months. When the fermentation is done, taste it and decide how you like it. It's nice dry. If you want it sweeter, stabilize it and sweeten it up a bit with a couple of ounces of dissolved sugar or boiled honey, and bottle it.

50.　　　Canned plum wine

- water, about $3\frac{1}{2}$ quarts
- 2 16 oz. (or so) cans of plums, any kind, in light syrup
- 2 lbs. sugar (if fruit is canned in heavy syrup, subtract another $\frac{1}{4}$ lb. of sugar; if canned in water, add $\frac{1}{4}$ lb.)
- 2 tsps. acid blend OR juice and zest of 2 lemons
- 1/8 tsp. tannin
- 1 tsp. yeast nutrient
- 1 Campden tablet, crushed (optional)
- $\frac{1}{2}$ tsp. pectic enzyme
- 1 packet Montrachet yeast

Heat the water. Drain the syrup from the fruit. Take out any pits, and place the fruit (and zest if you are using it) into a nylon straining bag. Put it in the bottom of a sanitized primary fermenter.

Measure out $3\frac{1}{2}$ quarts of warm water to start with, and add the fruit syrup. Add $1\frac{1}{2}$ pounds of the sugar and stir till dissolved. Be sure it is dissolved. Check the PA. For this wine you want about 12 percent potential alcohol.

If the PA is below 12 percent (and it probably will be), stir in the other $\frac{1}{2}$ pound of sugar. Stir it in well, and check the PA again. Don't worry if it is a degree off. The fruit still has sugar in it, too, don't forget.

Pour the water and sugar syrup mixture over the fruit, and add the lemon juice, if you are using it, or the acid, yeast nutrient, and tannin. After the must cools, add a crushed Campden tablet, if you choose to use one. Cover and fit with an air lock. Twelve hours after the Campden tablet, add the pectic enzyme. If you don't use the tablet, merely wait until the must cools down to add the pectic enzyme.

Twenty-four hours later, add the yeast.

Let it ferment for five days, stirring daily. When the PA falls to 3 to 4 percent, remove the fruit. Drain it well, but don't squeeze; it will simply turn to fine pulp that will displace the wine. Let the wine settle, then rack into a gallon jug. Bung and fit with an air lock.

Rack the wine once or twice over the next three to six months. When the fermentation is done, taste it and decide how you like it. If you want it sweeter, stabilize it and sweeten it up a bit with a couple of ounces of dissolved sugar or boiled honey, and bottle it.

CONCLUSION

Wine has been a staple of tables around the world for more than 4,000 years and in that time has developed into one of the most widely recognized and highly cultivated beverages in nearly every civilization on earth. From the rice wines of Asia to the grape wines of Europe or honey wines of Africa, wine is enjoyed by billions.

For that reason, many people seek out ways to make and enjoy their own wine from the comfort of their homes, growing their own grapes and experimenting with a wide array of ingredients to facilitate one of the world's oldest domestic processes.

With these straightforward recipes, making wine at home has never been easier!

Lightning Source UK Ltd.
Milton Keynes UK
UKHW020401030621
384806UK00001B/2